Toreadors wear tight-fitting suits embroidered with glittery silver and gold thread. They use a red cape to get the bull to charge, and a sword to kill it with. Can you spot the suit, the cape and the sword?

Olé.

Picasso painted bullfights many times. Here he draws the bull from different angles to show the movement of its head as it tosses the toreador into the air and on to its sharp horns.

Ouch!

Scène de Tauromachie was painted by Pablo Picasso in 1955.

Tipu's terrible tiger

This LARGE 'toy' was made for Tipu Sultan of Mysore who ruled in India about 200 years ago. Tipu was a brave warrior and his special sign was a fierce man-eating tiger. His weapons, throne and buildings were all decorated with tiger stripes.

Tipu hated the British army who were fighting in India. So he had this toy made that shows a tiger eating a soldier.

Very, very scary!

Just imagine what it was like to have a huge toy that made horrible noises! Eeeeek!

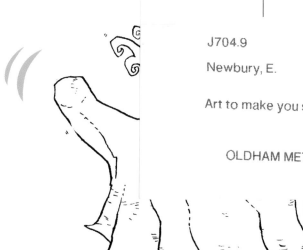

Elizabeth Newbery

F
FRANCES LINCOLN
CHILDREN'S BOOKS

Blood and guts!

Pablo Picasso was born in Spain. Like many Spaniards, he loved to watch bullfighting – a very **dangerous** sport. The fighters, called toreadors, try to kill fierce black bulls – but they are often badly injured or killed too.

Tipu loved technology and gadgets.
A mini organ was hidden inside
the tiger. When Tipu turned
the handle, the tiger ROARED.

ROARR
ROARR
ROARR

Tipu's Tiger was made of painted wood in about 1795.

Danger at sea

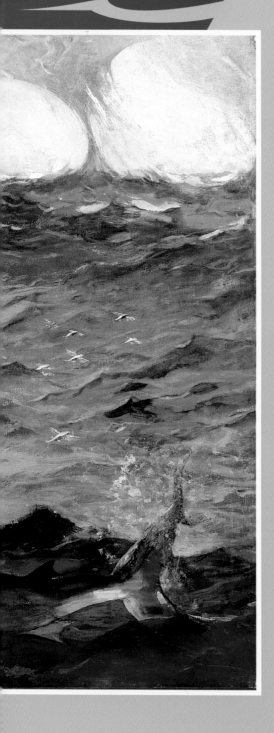

This painting is about a **terrible accident** about to happen. Look how the stormy sea is tossing the tiny boat around. The mast and bowsprit have snapped off and the sails are down, so the sailor has no control over the boat. In the distance there's a waterspout – and it's right on course to hit the boat. Some very, very hungry sharks are closing in for the KILL!

Look! I can see a tiny ship on the horizon. Is it going to rescue the sailor?

Winslow Homer painted many pictures of the sea, divers and fishermen. He liked to show the struggle between people and nature.

The Gulf Stream was painted by Winslow Homer in 1899.

What a fright!

Do you draw pictures of horrible monsters? Have you ever wondered what would happen if they could spring to life? Well, Maryama Okyo made pictures so real that they looked as though they would come alive. Heeeeelp!

Maryama lived in Japan about 200 years ago and he was especially well known for his paintings of spooky ghosts. Much later, another Japanese artist, Tsukioka Yoshitoshi, made this picture. He makes fun of Maryama by showing the artist painting a ghost so real that it comes alive. It rears up out of the picture and frightens the artist out of his wits!

BOOOO!

Okyo Paints A Ghost is a woodcut made by Tsukioka Yoshitoshi in 1882.

Bones and teeth

This is the mask of Tezcatlipoca. He was a god worshipped by the Aztecs who lived in Mexico about 500 years ago.

Tezcatlipoca was the god of darkness, magic, war and death. He had a mirror that gave off a special smoke to kill his enemies.

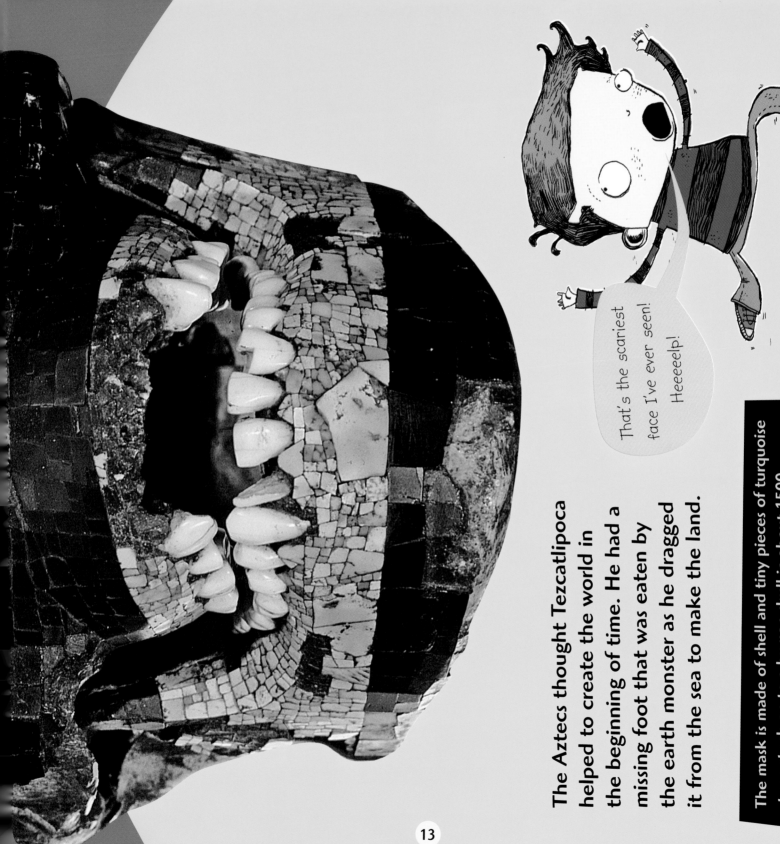

That's the scariest face I've ever seen! Heeeeelp!

The Aztecs thought Tezcatlipoca helped to create the world in the beginning of time. He had a missing foot that was eaten by the earth monster as he dragged it from the sea to make the land.

The mask is made of shell and tiny pieces of turquoise stone stuck on to a human skull in about 1500.

Charge!

Scotland Forever was painted by Elizabeth Thompson in 1881.

When this picture was painted in Victorian times, most pictures of war showed big views of battlefields or officers doing brave deeds. Elizabeth Thompson wanted to show people what war was like for ordinary soldiers.

She painted this scene of the Battle of Waterloo long after it happened. To show how terrifying it was to attack in battle she got soldiers to charge at her as she sat at her easel! Then soldiers posed for her wearing their uniforms so that she could get the details right.

These horses look as though they're coming right out of the picture.

They look as if they're going to crash into each other.

A strange spell

Do you ever have weird dreams? This painting is a little bit like a strange dream. Look at the snake charmer. Is it a man or a made-up creature? What is he wearing? Does he make you feel uneasy? He is certainly charming the snakes. How many can you spot slithering out?

Can you spot anything else in the jungle?

The air seems very still and quiet. Do you think the snake charmer has put a spell on all the other animals, birds and plants too?

Last night I dreamt . . .

16

The Snake Charmer was painted by Henri Rousseau in 1907.

A very fishy tale

This is a page from a book made over 700 years ago. It shows the tale of a cunning sea monster who liked to trick sailors into thinking it was an island.

Two Fishermen on a Sea Creature was painted about 1270.

What a nasty fish!

I think it's a whale.

The giant fish would keep very still with its huge back just above the water. Passing sailors would think it was an island. They would pitch a camp on its back and light a fire.

When the sea monster felt the heat of the camp-fire, it would suddenly plunge to the bottom of the ocean, drowning the poor sailors. What a mean thing to do!

More about the art and artists

● *Scène de Tauromachie* by **Pablo Picasso** is painted with oil paints. It is in a private collection.

Pablo Picasso was born in Malaga, Spain in 1881 and died in 1973. Although he was Spanish, he lived and worked in France for most of his life. Picasso made thousands of drawings and paintings. He also decorated pots, made sculptures, designed stage and film sets and made prints too. Many people think he was the greatest artist of the 20th century.

● *Tipu's Tiger* can be seen in the Victoria and Albert Museum, London. Sadly, we don't know the names of the craftspeople who built the tiger.

Sultan Tipu was killed in a great battle against the British in India. Lord Clive was in charge of the British Army. After Tipu's death, he was given some of Tipu's things, including the tiger.

● *The Gulf Stream* by **Winslow Homer** is painted with oil paints. You can see it in The Metropolitan Museum of Art, New York.

Winslow Homer was born in Boston, USA in 1836 and died in 1910. When he was a boy, Winslow lived by the sea. He knew what fun it is to swim, paddle and play in the sea. But look at his painting on page 8 and 9 again. Do you think he knew how frightening the sea could be in a big storm?

● *Okyo Paints A Ghost* is a woodcut made by **Tsukioka Yoshitoshi** in 1882. There are prints of the picuture all over the world.

Tsukioka was born in 1839 and died in 1892. He was a very famous woodcut artist. (A woodcut is a bit like a potato print except that the pattern or picture is cut out of wood, not a potato.)

In Tsukioka's day, Shinto was the main religion of Japan. People believed that the ghosts of dead people came back to haunt the living. So you'll find lots of ghosts in Japanese art.

● Look for the **mask of Tezcatlipoca** in the British Museum. We don't know who made it but they were very skilled. The Aztecs believed that their gods only rewarded human beings if they were offered human blood. So people were sacrificed as food for the gods.

Although the Aztec religion seems savage to us, the people were well educated. Many could read and write. They were very skilled craftspeople, astronomers and mathematicians. They invented the calendar and wrote down their history before many other people in ancient South America.

● *Scotland Forever* by **Elizabeth Thompson** was painted in oil paints. You can see it in Leeds City Art Gallery.

Elizabeth Thompson was born in 1846 and died in 1933. She painted battle scenes from her imagination. When she married Major William Butler she travelled with him to countries at war. She painted real battles and her paintings became very popular. Later, people thought that her pictures showed the horrors of war so well that men were frightened to join the army! Then she found it difficult to sell her paintings.

● *The Snake Charmer* is painted in oil paints by **Henri Rousseau**. You can see it in the Musée d'Orsay, Paris.

Henri was born in 1844 in Laval, France and died in 1910. He worked for the Paris customs office and taught himself to paint. Henri is best known for his jungle pictures he said were painted in Mexico but were really taken from magazines and trips to the zoo and museums.

● *Two Fishermen on a Sea Creature* is a page from a book about tales of real and imaginary animals. You can see it in the J. Paul Getty Museum, Los Angeles. It was made in Europe in the Middle Ages but we don't know the name of the artist who illustrated it.

The book is made of parchment (the skin of a goat). The pictures in the book are decorated with real gold so it must have been made for a very important person.

PHOTOGRAPHIC ACKNOWLEDGMENTS

For permission to reproduce the works of art shown on the following pages
and for supplying images, the Publishers would like to thank:

© Asian Art and Archaeology, Inc./CORBIS: front cover and 10–11
British Museum/Werner Forman Archive: 12–13
J. Paul Getty Museum, Los Angeles (83.MR.173): 18–19
© Leeds Museums and Galleries (City Art Gallery)/www.bridgeman.co.uk: 14–15
Photograph © 1995 The Metropolitan Museum of Art: 8–9 (Catharine Lorillard Wolfe Collection, Wolfe Fund, 1906. 06.1234)
Musée d'Orsay, Paris/www.bridgeman.co.uk: 16–17
© Succession Picasso/DACS 2007/www.bridgeman.co.uk: 4–5
V&A Images/Victoria and Albert Museum: 6–7

First published in Great Britain in 2007 and in the USA in 2008
by Frances Lincoln Children's Books, 4 Torriano Mews,
Torriano Avenue, London NW5 2RZ
www.franceslincoln.com

British Library Cataloguing in Publication Data
available on request

ISBN: 978-1-84507-584-2

Printed in Singapore

9 8 7 6 5 4 3 2 1